POPPING
Your Marketing
CHERRY

A Book on How to Get Your
Budding Business to Go All the Way

Alicia Williams
founder of Aliste Marketing, Inc

Aliste Marketing
300 W Main Street
Northborough, MA 029103
www.alistemarketing.com

ISBN-13 # 978-0692520178

Cover and book design by Betsy Stepp, Fiddlehead Graphic Design
NEWTON'S CRADLE: ZENTILIA/123RF; CHERRY: MIKEEW/ISTOCK

Acknowledgements to our editor Katie Fagan

This book is dedicated to all of the amazing entrepreneurs that have crossed my path, mentors that have guided me through this journey, and my family who never got off this train ride with me!

Table of Contents

Introduction

I know, I know. With a title like **Popping Your Marketing Cherry**, I totally get what you're thinking: "Oh, great. Here's *another* marketing book I should slug through to finally launch my brilliant idea..." (Wait, no. Get your mind out of the gutter if you were thinking this was about something else!). And, I'll give it to you. If this were any other marketing book, I'd say you'd be right—except for one, big difference: this book is 100% no nonsense. Promise! So say *sayonara* to traditional marketing terminology and industry jargon, and say *what's up* to **The Aliste Way**—a straightforward, no B.S. approach that will **actually** teach you (yes, YOU) how to get your product and/or services in front of those that want and need them.

So why did I write "another" marketing book? Because when I set out to create my own marketing business, **Aliste Marketing**, I buried myself in hundreds of industry-related texts to try and learn how to successfully market my new venture (read: total mind screw!). I poured over pages and pages about traditional marketing, guerilla marketing, grassroots marketing, marketing for dummies, marketing for moms, marketing for marketing, and...well, you get the picture. So you'd think that, after learning about all the ideas within these books, that I'd have "it." You know, that "I'm ready to tackle the world" feeling of total and utter know-how. But the problem was that the ideas in those books where just that. Ideas. What I needed then (and know *every* business needs still) were **strategies**. Deep down, I felt I should be aspiring to something more than just the standard "ordering hundreds of business cards and leaving them at restaurants, cleaners, libraries, churches, etc." approach. What I wanted (and craved!) was a marketing book that offered a strategy for getting people to not only contact *my business* but, to sign on the dotted line, as well. Hence why I had to write this book—to give you, the budding business owner, a strategy that actually works!

And I've made it super **easy**. This book is divided step-by-step into five fun chapters to help you adapt **The Aliste Way** into your business's marketing strategy. At the end of each chapter you'll find a workbook section set up to help your business fill in the blanks and find "The One," that perfect audience. So, take a breath, pour yourself a glass of vino, and get ready for a journey filled with lots of *ah ha!* moments and plenty of *oh, yeah's!*

Finding the Perfect Match

How to Capture the Attention of Your Brilliant Ideas

Be Your Own Matchmaker: The Top Three Traits

How to Capture the Attention of Your Brilliant Ideas

Let's face it. Ideas can be like an awful relationship (read: totally flaky). One minute they're all "I'm here for you!" and the next, they're running for the hills. To make my bond with my ideas more fitting (because they are, after all, the yeast to an entrepreneur's bread and butter), I sleep with a notebook next to my bed, have another one that lives in my car, and tote around several straggling pieces of paper in my purse—at. all. times. Why? Because ideas seem to come at the most *random* moments, and capturing those special ones to see how we can build off of them is where our creativity really has the chance to shine. They are the seeds to our budding businesses; are they not?

So how can you get your ideas to work *for* you instead of against you? Well, just like in love, you've got to always be ready for them! When I met my husband, we were in high school (I know right?). But imagine if I hadn't been open to the idea of dating him because I was too scared, too busy, too lazy, too [insert closed-off excuse here] to try and capture his attention? I may have never had the chance to marry him.

Similarly you've got to be open to capturing your come-as-they-will ideas—preferably with *plenty* of notebooks and recording devices around. If you *think* you're not ready to take on that brilliant idea and you let it pass you by (because you're sure you'll remember it later...), it could just wind up being *The One That Got Away* instead of *The One*.

Be Your Own Matchmaker:
The Top Three Traits

"Matchmaker, matchmaker, make me a match!
Find me a find, catch me a catch!"

- Fiddler on the Roof

Okay, get this tune *out* of your head—fast. And stop being so expectant of others. That great idea you've got your eye on, well it won't ever land its first date with the "perfect match" (a.k.a. your **target consumer audience**) if you're relying on the idea to do all the work for you. A fabulous idea—while totally fabulous—doesn't guarantee your target audience will come running to find it. To be successful, your businesses must market based on specific **strategies** instead of just top-of-mind ideas. And I know. It's a tough pill to swallow after you've gotten good and excited about your new idea! But humble yourself, grasshopper. Just like in love, you need to "know thy self" before you'll ever know The One.

Still not sure what I'm getting at? Here's another way to look at it: you're single and hoping to be married in the near future. So you blind date. And blind date. And blind date. But instead of figuring out exactly what you want in a partner (like, say, someone who loves dogs that you could easily meet volunteering at a local shelter!) you give up, completely exhausted and reconsidering relationships altogether…let alone *marriage.* Your dating attempts have failed, even though you know you have so much to offer.

Marketing works the same way. If you don't know enough about your idea or product's purpose, you won't be able to make a successful match with potential customers. And that will leave you *and* your business defeated. That's why we need to stop looking for love in all the wrong places. Instead, we must become our own successful matchmakers by asking these three questions of the *who*, the *what*, and the *how* to putting a successful strategy in motion. Without these three, we're just shooting blind on a hunch that the idea will work.

Who needs it?

Looking at your business, think about how your services, offerings or products help the end user, a.k.a. your "perfect match."

What does it solve?

Every business and product must solve a problem in order for a customer or client to click "Buy Now." Look at your ideal customer/client and understand how your idea/business simplifies their life, increases their bottom-line, fills their stomach, etc.

How does it help?

Describe your ideal client—what do they look like, think like, read, talk about, etc. Really visualize them. Understand what in their life makes them need your business or products and exactly how your brand will help solve that need.

Ideas and businesses do well when they solve a **need**. People buy what they see as desirable or what they see as a necessity. Think of the electric car. It solved a need for eco-friendly, cash-conscious, and tech-savvy consumers alike. They each wanted a car that decreased their carbon footprint, limited their spending on gas, and demonstrated technological innovation. The electric car **solved** the needs of these target markets that the average automobile was lacking.

Similarly, when I had the idea to write this book, I asked those same questions of myself prior to moving forward (because *no* company is above playing their own matchmaker). Here's how it all played out:

Who needs it?

Business owners, entrepreneurs, and individuals who need to understand how to begin marketing their ideas, products, and/or services to grow their businesses.

What does this solve?

While I wish I could say it solved something more important like World Peace, the reality is that this book was designed to provide a marketing blueprint for readers looking to build a brand and market its product or service. And who knows, maybe that *could* help someone else campaign for World Peace–so here's to hoping.

How does it help?

Not only was the need *so* real for my own business, but I've heard countless others speak to the overwhelming bombardment of "information" out there on how to market–the multiple theories, ever-changing social platforms, varying consulting advice, and everything in between–wishing for an effective and simplified approach to marketing.

Without these questions, the odds that I'd get this book into your hands would have greatly diminished. Largely because I probably wouldn't have fully understood exactly who you are and what you need!

Just like dating, you can't expect to build a business on a great, money-making idea without thinking hard about your mission first. You have to really love and believe in what you're doing— and the only way to do that is to *know* every inch of what that is. True success is **knowing** yourself and your passions, and how those align with your brand and your mission. Oh, and using sound marketing strategies (for which we've got you covered) to make that "happily ever after" come true.

Work It Out

Let's get started:

How will you plan to capture your ideas?

Your business/product/service is:

Who needs this?

What does it solve?

How does this help?

Bonus Q

When does your ideal client use this business/product/service?

CHAPTER

2

Landing the First Date

Your New Marketing 101

How to Woo
Potential Prospects

How to Make a
Swoon-Worthy Ask

Your New Marketing 101

I think we can all agree on this: no one and I mean no one is attracted to desperation. If you're overeager, you can come off as pushy or obnoxious which can be a total turn off—making it really tough to land a first date with anyone. So when it comes to connecting with your potential customers, be real. Instead of pushing your product, appeal to the customer's needs (you know, those we established in Chapter 1) and sweep them off their damn feet! Because once you've made that all-important first impression, then you've got the opportunity to go in for the ask. So here's your New Marketing 101: first woo your customer and *then* make the ask. It's that simple!

How to Woo
Potential Prospects

No one wants to be sold to. We get enough of that as it is—when we walk through the mall we're chased with perfume, or fast food clerks who upsell to the larger size for "just fifty cents more," and looking at cars? Ugh, forget it! This approach to marketing looks far too much like the person whose dating advice is "Keep asking, someone's bound to say yes!" In theory, it sounds successful, but the reality is that it's just downright desperate... not to mention exhausting for the asker and the askee. So break out of that cycle by learning to relate to your customer as a person instead of a consumer before you make the big ask—it'll save you time and energy to boot!

It's in our nature to support those that we trust to make us feel safe and special. Think of the auto repair shop that offers Wi-Fi and coffee while you get an oil change, or even the local cafe you frequent because they're dog friendly. You support them because they go out of their way to make you feel special, right? That extra effort is what instills trust in our business and allows clients to feel safe. Now think of that coffee shop that adds cream every time you ask for sugar only, the computer shop that makes returns a nightmare, or the restaurant that *always* forgets your reservation—there's no way you'll continue to support them with that type of action or behavior, because they've proven you can't rely on them to make you feel special or safe.

At its core, marketing is performing an action in order to elicit a measurable response. Each move a marketer makes should aim to make a potential customer feel *special*. So really, it's that feeling—that "special"—that is marketing. I mean, no one wakes up eager "to market." I *love* marketing and even I don't jump out of bed and say, "Let's market!" Instead, I wake up and list what I'm going to do that day: "I'm going to call three prospects, apply to give eight presentations, finish Aliste's website, write a blog, post on social media..." and the list goes on. But all of those actions don't become "marketing" unless they result in a measurable response:

- ☑ By calling three prospects and asking for the sale, I closed three deals.

- ☑ With the submission of my speaker kit, I secured eight presentations.

- ☑ In finishing Aliste's website, I brought credibility to my business.

- ☑ Through consistently writing blogs and updates, I reaffirmed my social media presence.

All of those actions became marketing when they did what I wanted them to do, a.k.a. get my business closer to our target market audience by building a stronger relationship with them.

- ☑ By calling three prospects and asking for the sale, I made new clients feel special by reaching out to them instead of having them come to me.

- ☑ By submitting my speaker kit, I demonstrated my skills as a valuable marketer worthy of presenting to my industry, which exposes me as an authority to new audiences/potential client relationships.

- ☑ In finishing Aliste's website, I brought credibility to my business by providing current and potential customers with a transparent informational hub on my company.

- ☑ By consistently writing blogs and updates, I reaffirmed my social media presence so that current and potential customers can get to know me and trust me.

Those actions, little by little, build on one another to make up the bigger picture that is marketing—actions that elicit a measureable response. So how and where *does* one even begin when it comes to asking, measuring and working up the courage to make a successful ask?

How to Make a Swoon-Worthy Ask

When we go to networking events we have no issue standing up, giving our sixty second sell, and making the ask. Unlike the unnerving moment of having to ask a love interest to dinner for the first time (lots of pressure to make them feel special!), networking more closely resembles attending the likes of a cocktail party, where the pressure and focus is totally off the ask itself. In that environment you can be free to "do you" if, and when, the opportunity arises for an ask:

> *"Hi, my name is John. I'm a foodie enthusiast with a restaurant review service and today I'm looking to be connected with your local pizza shop."*

Yet, when it comes to our own marketing, both in print and online, we tend to get bashful and forget the ask. As business owners, entrepreneurs, and marketers, the ask is the most important piece of any marketing material. The ask doesn't have to be and shouldn't be a "Buy Here, Buy Now" approach. But it must be clear enough that your potential customer doesn't need a third party to read between the lines of your advertisement.

So let's take a look at a few examples of the dos and don'ts of how to make that swoon-worthy ask:

DON'T Get Caught up in the Promotion

ABC Landscape is a small landscaping business that currently thrives with their lawn-mowing services in spring, their busiest season. However, they want to increase fall cleanup among these existing customers and recruit new prospects to boost their slowest season, Fall. Thus, ABC has created a promotion—*20% Off Fall Clean Ups*—and sent it out through their existing social media pages, created an email-specific campaign, and invested in direct mailings to target neighborhoods. So what are they missing?

ABC Landscaping is so driven by the promotional element that they forgot to address all three important questions (from Chapter 1) to help build a proper marketing message:

☑ **Who needs this?**   Property owners

☐ **What does this solve?**   ?

☐ **How does this help?**   ?

As a potential customer, I don't want to see the "Buy Here, Buy Now" approach that they've taken with their current 20% off notification (because no one likes being told how to spend their money). Instead, I want to know *why* I need ABC Landscape to clean up my leaves—nature put them there for a reason, after all! So what's the big deal if I don't clean them up? What I need to know, as a potential buyer, are the benefits of using ABC Landscape, the company history, and the value of their service.

How can we turn this *don't* into a *do*? Take the two minutes required to consider all three questions (from Chapter 1) and see how the answers change the marketing efforts from a loss to a win:

☑ **Who needs this?**   Property owners

☑ **What does this solve?**   Eliminates the damaging effects of compiling leaves which, if left untouched until spring, would damage and ultimately kill the property's lawn, resulting in more money spent on chemicals used to revive it come spring.

☑ **How does this help?**

On average, homeowners spend between $200-500 for leaf removal services compared to the average lawn fertilization services (based on an acre of land) for $3,662.63. So homeowners would save over $3,000 dollars with this service.[1]

DO Highlight Why It's Needed

Okay, so now that we have all three questions answered, let's see how we can change the marketing message to show the value of using ABC Landscape instead of focusing too closely on only the promotion.

Here's what the original promotion (*20% off Fall Clean Up*) looks like *after* we incorporate the WHY into the messaging:

> *Save* **over** *$3,000 dollars with our fall clean up service and enjoy a beautiful lawn this spring! Call 1-800-ABC-Lands to book now.*
> *mention this ad and receive 20% off*

See what we did there? We showed the **value** of the service (saving *over* $3,000), the **benefits** of fall clean up (enjoying a beautiful lawn come spring) and made a clear **call to action** (Call 1-800-ABC-Lands), a.k.a. the ask. By encouraging readers to mention the 20% discount from the advertisement, we're *also* **measuring** the response of our initial action (sending the message out via email, social media, and direct mailing) and are, thus, truly marketing! Now that's some hot stuff.

---

[1] *Leaf removal and lawn fertilization services from www.homeadvisor.com*

Work It Out

Now add up your own formula:

The Ask Formula

value added **+** service **+** benefits of using service **+** call to action
*bonus for measuring response **= YES**

value added: _____ service: _____

benefits: _____ call to action: _____

bonus for measuring response: _____

Examples:

Save time with our dog walking service and enjoy an evening with a tired and happy best friend. Email sally@dogwalkingisawesome.com to schedule your pup's walk.

Crazy with holiday shopping? Let our professional shoppers make you the hero of the holidays with gorgeous gift wrapped presents right from your wish list. Start relaxing now by registering online at wemakeiteasy.abc

Okay, now try it for your business!

Save _____ on _____
      VALUE   SERVICE

and enjoy _____!
              BENEFIT

_____ today!
          CALL TO ACTION

* _____
        BONUS OF OPTION FOR MEASURING RESPONSE

3

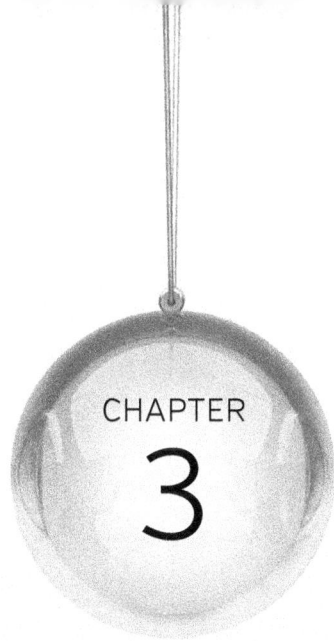

Getting Real Before the "I Do"

Learn to Be Vulnerable

Get to Know the
***Real** Marketing*

Learn to Be Vulnerable

Recently my husband and I went to a comedy show (it's kind of our thing—hello, date night!). We get such a kick out of seeing a comedian stand up and poke fun at the everyday mundane, saying all the things we think but never have the guts to speak aloud. And it got me thinking...what if we approached marketing the same way? Okay, maybe not *exactly* the same way—some comedians can be pretty harsh! But, regardless of whether they're vulgar or clean, the one thing they all do have in common is that they're honest and totally upfront. They own it. That's their story and they're sticking to it!

When I first started Aliste Marketing, I was guilty of not telling my story—at the time, I didn't want people to know that I was such a newbie. I was only twenty-one when I set out. Twenty-one! Today, the fact that I started my business the day after I graduated college (with zero investors and employees) is a huge asset in making my business relatable to target clients. We all have to start somewhere, right? And many of my clients have either started the same way or just need that "if she can do it, I can do it!" kind of motivation to turn their idea into a six figure business.

And while it may feel scary to open up like that—like when you finally let your new significant other in on your childhood snuggle buddy (I'm talking about you, Mr. Teddy!)—it's absolutely worth it. No, in fact, it's necessary. Because you can't hide who you (or Mr. Teddy) are forever. So get used to that vulnerability. *Own* your story. And get comfortable sharing it with the world. Because people want to hear about you—they want to be able to relate to you, your business, and your mission. Because we all want someone we feel akin to and believe in.

Point and case: **Capital One Spark** actually picked up my story (once I got comfortable owning it) and highlighted Aliste's success in their **Spark Entrepreneur** series [see below]. Just by being my authentic self and telling my story, I've found yet another avenue to relate to my audience all while spreading the word about my mission. Win-win!

So, let's hear your story. Submit the answers to this chapter's *Work It Out* page for an opportunity to be showcased on our blog and social media channels!

What is your story? Contact us at **MyStory@alistemarketing.com** to be featured on our blog and marketing channels.

Get to Know the *Real* Marketing

Get real. *No, literally—get real.* It's all too easy to see through the bullshit these days (remember, that's why I wrote this book in the first place) and that's why getting real and being vulnerable is so important. It's truly a key element to good marketing—*real* marketing. It not only helps you better understand what you're trying to offer (by being honest with yourself about it first), but it also helps your audience understand it. Because life's too short to be something you're not. In the end, it will just confuse people. Kind of like when you find out your love interest prefers blondes, so you dye your hair a horribly, trendy bright yellow and then *no one* recognizes you. You're not fooling anyone...other than perhaps just making a fool of yourself!

Similarly, the other week I was watching television and saw a car commercial with the slogan, *when you want anything but predicable.* I totally lost it! My husband just stared blankly as I tried to explain to him—between belly laughs—my take on the commercial. I mean, hello! The *one* thing in my life I need to be predictable is my car. I need to know that my car will get me safely to work in the morning, and at 5pm when the day is over, it will also get me safely home. I couldn't relate to the tagline so I dismissed even the thought of being a consumer or believer in what they were selling. The unpredictable car? Yeah, not for me—or most folks, I would imagine. This company didn't appear to really understand how their mission related to those they were selling to!

On the other hand, **Stella Artois** recently released a campaign for their signature lager titled, *"Buy a Lady a Drink."* Okay, now *that's* brilliant. Naturally, I could relate—and I'm not even a beer drinker! Instead, I was fascinated with their campaign's **mission**. As a result, I wound up telling all my family and friends about this amazing campaign. Their mission is to raise awareness and funding for providing clean water in developing countries. How cool is that? Not only does it help to promote their golden brew—and its main ingredient, water—but it also helps to support a great humanitarian cause. If you've got a minute, I highly encourage you to watch the video at www.buyaladyadrink.com to see its effects, and that's some free promotion right there.

What's a small business like you to do when you don't have the campaign budget of a national car company or world-renowned beer company? It's easier than you think. Just pull back the curtains, get real, and show who you really are as a business and culture. Stop trying to do as the big wigs do when that's not what you are (yet...). As small businesses, we've got such a personal advantage over the larger corporations—who so frequently try to position themselves as small and local like us—so why not take advantage of it? Get your mission out there. And get marketing!

Work It Out

Now it's time to get comfortable letting your guard down and telling your authentic story by answering these questions:

Why did you start your own company or choose your current career?

_____

_____

Fill in the blank:

My management style is _____ .

What keeps you up at night?

_____

_____

What adjectives would you use to describe entrepreneurship or your personality?

_____

_____

If you had another career what would it be and why?

_____

_____

Define "success." What does it mean to you?

_____

_____

Where do you see yourself in five years?

_____

_____

Meeting the Family

How to Win Them Over

Fit Right In

How to Win Them Over

Dating has changed drastically in just the last decade. Thanks to apps like Tinder, websites like Match.com, and countless other online resources, now we rely on social media to meet our future spouses or leave it to algorithms to bring our soul mates directly into our inbox. Instead of *You've Got Mail* it should say *You've Got A Soul Mate*!

What happens when your idea does finally make that connection with your target audience and you're now ready for them to "meet the family"?

Well, just like the change in the dating scene (want to meet my mom on Skype?), we've seen a huge switch on how we talk to prospects, customers, and our target audience in marketing. Naturally marketing has changed in order to adapt to our cultural social media focus.

Traditionally we think of sales as a funnel where the varying widths represent the varying amounts of time, money, and energy spent on marketing to new and/or current customers. Typically, the widest end of the funnel represents the most efforts spent on converting **new** prospects into current customers, and the narrowest end represents the least efforts spent on retaining **current** customers—mostly operating under the assumption "once a beloved customer, always a beloved customer."

Which sounds like it makes total sense. Why spend the *most* amount of time on people who already love your brand when there is a whole, huge market of those who still have yet to meet you?

Have you ever purchased cable before? You buy in when there's an attractive promotion and then lo and behold three months later your bill is suddenly *way* higher. But when you call to dispute the charges, you're told that the promotion was only for **new** customers. You're now **old** news (see what I did there?). Because the longer you're a customer the more you have to pay—that's how the funnel system really works. Which *doesn't* make sense!

What if you chose to treat your significant other *family* like that? Yikes! Can you imagine? If, after getting the stamp of approval, you decide you're "in" and blow them off for the rest of the relationship. You are bound to cause major, unwanted family drama and that good favor you were so sure would always last; it's gonzo.

How do we solve this problem? Flip the funnel! When we use new marketing tools, like email marketing, social media platforms, event planning, and online surveys, we maintain special, *focused* contact with the people who already know, love, support, and believe in our business and mission—a.k.a. our family! So if the top of the funnel now represents the majority of our money, time, and energy focused on staying in touch with our quality contacts, and the least amount of money, time, and energy on finding strangers to buy into our mission, then we're keeping *everyone* smiling.

But, what about those strangers, you ask? Well, for the sake of our metaphor, let's think of those strangers as distant family or close family friends. Their favor definitely still matters and *will* affect your relationship. Why? Because the family's going to talk about you to them—whether it's good or bad. And that could be the difference between having a whole slew of fans in your corner or none at all.

That's why it's crucial to flip the funnel and put the majority of your efforts towards making current customers (the family) happy, since what a real person has to say about your business holds more value than *any* shiny advertisement. This way you grow your contact base and profits through repeat business and referrals from the inside out.

And that's how tons of major brands are using social media to their advantage—**engagement marketing** converts prospects into supporters thanks to their current followers. And for the first time in marketing, the company is in direct, real-time dialogue with its customer by commenting on Facebook, retweeting on Twitter, or posting snapshots on Instagram. In this way, businesses allow customers to feel involved and be engaged—which is what any family member wants, after all.

Fit Right In

We all know looks aren't everything. Although appearances can help you to fit in (and may even have their own, different kind of "wow" factor), when it comes to meeting the family the real "wow" factor that counts is making them feel **special** (remember Chapter 3). While your business may have an amazing cover photo, professional logo and template designs, and a world class website, if your customer experience doesn't provide that "wow" effect, it all falls short—way too short to successfully build your business.

But the best part about getting that "wow" effect? It doesn't have to cost you a dime! It can be something as simple as saying "Welcome to Moe's" or singing "Happy Birthday" to a celebrating customer.

Let's take a look at how that "wow" factor works in the real world. **PRIME Your Trusted Butcher,** one of our clients, is a local butcher shop in direct competition with the big grocers in the area. They created a "wow" factor that would make them stand out from the larger, cookie-cutter chains. And because we know that a customer who has a poor experience is going to give warning to their friends and family, we also know the same will hold true if they have a positive "wow" experience.

Here is the formula we use at Aliste for understanding how that "wow" experience translates into not only new prospects, but happy current customers, too!

➡ Provide a "wow" experience.

➡ Encourage your customers to stay in touch and share their experience through social media.

➡ Engage with customers to gain visibility and expand your network, while driving new prospects in the door.

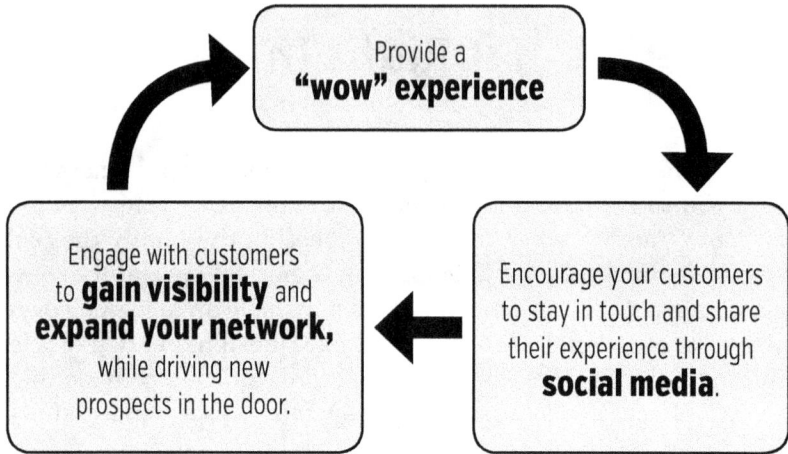

Provide a
"wow" experience

Engage with customers
to **gain visibility** and
expand your network,
while driving new
prospects in the door.

Encourage your customers
to stay in touch and share
their experience through
social media.

With PRIME, they wanted to make an impact the second a customer walked through the door. As a result, they broke down the "wow" factor into a series of steps to elicit that "wow" moment:

★ **Get the customer's attention:** *"Hi, welcome to PRIME!"*

★ **Create a personal connection:** *"I'm Matt, your local butcher. What are you cooking for dinner tonight?"*

★ **Engage the customer as a specific individual:** Suggest appropriate wine pairings and/or recipe recommendations depending on customer response.

★ **Add the service touch:** Walk customer over to the checkout counter and make the ask—*"Sign up for our newsletter?"*

This approach aims to delightfully surprise the customer (the woo!), who more often than not just feels like another number at other deli counters, by engaging with them on a personal, customized level. After successfully delighting them, only then does the butcher make the ask for continued engagement with their newsletter updates (to review the woo and the ask, visit Chapter 3). And this happy, unique "wow" factor experience will be shared. How do I know that? Because, thanks to the internet and social media, we live in a world where sharing is *everything*. Which is why that initial, personal engagement from the business is likely to be returned with an online engagement from the customer—be it sharing pictures from company events, posting testimonials or tweeting their experience—which can all be seen by their powerful network of potential customers.

You can (and should!) include a "wow" factor, too—think about one little change you can make, or emphasize something you're already doing, so it becomes that "wow" experience to drive engagement and allow you to flip the funnel. It's how you get an "I'm thrilled to finally meet you! I've heard *so* many good things" instead of an "Oh, you're *Jo's* fiancé? Excuse me, I've got to use the bathroom" (because, awkwarddd!) at that next family gathering.

Work It Out

Wondering how to create that "wow" experience? The best place to start is by looking at how other companies have created it for you by answering these four questions:

What companies do you love supporting?

_____

_____

_____

_____

What was the "wow" experience they offered?

_____

_____

_____

_____

What do you currently do in your business that competitors don't?

_____

_____

_____

_____

How can you make one change to set yourself apart? (i.e. personally introduce yourself, send a thank you card, a small gift, etc.)

_____

_____

_____

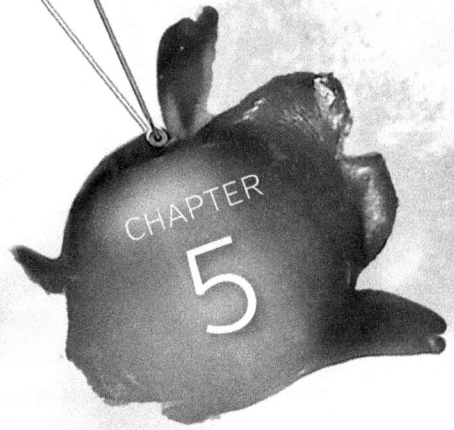

Hearing Wedding Bells

Hearing "I Do"

Honeymoon Content

Planning for the Future

Growing Your Family

Hearing "I Do"

Email marketing and other social media channels are just channels until we wed them with an effective marketing strategy. Your channels need to say "I do" to that strategy to prove they're in a committed relationship towards pushing your brand's mission and online presence. And if these channels and strategies aren't working together, they're simply ships passing in the night.

Or planes forever circling in the night. Imagine Boston's Logan Airport. The airlines don't actually make any money unless they dock at Logan, pick up passengers, and bring them to their final destinations. At Aliste, we look at our marketing the same way—we have our website (Logan airport) which is the hub of all our business information and social media outlets. We've got a Facebook plane, a Twitter plane, and an email marketing plane all circling around, waiting to land with passengers they've picked up from around the internet world. And if they don't land (a.k.a. bring that social media following/traffic to your website), they won't actually make our business any money. We need tourists!

Feel like traveling? Because it's time for your honeymoon!

Honeymoon Content

Content is one of the strongest ways a business can establish a credible presence, provide a valuable resource to attract new customers, and reward a loyal following. And don't sweat it if you're not a writer. That's totally okay! Just be sure to find someone who *is* and begin creating that original content which will live on your website through blogs. Then reinforce that content through social media posts and in email marketing campaigns (ah, wedded bliss!).

And, hey, feel free to take the whole month for your honeymoon. A single blog can provide one month's worth of content for both your newsletter and social media pages! Believe that?

However, I encourage you to think long and hard about what your business and team can **consistently** commit to outside of regular blog posting. This is marriage people—commitment is a big deal, so be honest about it! It's super easy to get wrapped up in the latest and greatest social media platforms, but if you neglect them, they'll only wind up hurting your credibility instead of bolstering it.

I'd recommend only picking **two platforms**/channels you feel really comfortable and excited about to start, and only adding more when it is right for your business. If you can only dedicate yourself (or a team) to write a weekly blog, then focus on the blog and do it really well. And once you've got that comfortably mastered then, and only then, would I suggest adding in that quarterly e-book you've had your sights on. Because being a jack-of-all-trades results in a master of none. So start small, plan well, and *then* grow!

Planning for the Future

Fail to plan, plan to fail. It's one of my favorite sayings — because achieving success doesn't happen by accident! It happens because you prepped, previewed, and worked your butt off to make it happen. Especially when you've got a lot of moving pieces on your plate.

Let's take a sneak peek into how we plan for the future at Aliste.

First, you've got to be able to elaborate on these three areas:

Marketing Goals: What are your goals?

To increase overall brand exposure and credibility.

Purpose of Content: How can this content achieve our goal?

Drive repeat visitors to website and social pages, enforce validation and credibility within the industry, increase name recognition/search optimization.

Measuring Success: All marketing has to be measurable — what milestones will show the success or failure of our actions?

Conversion, traffic increase, improved listings, time on website, repeat visitors, downloads and subscriptions.

Secondly, you'll need to create a content plan or checklist for your different channels or outlets (make sure you have **at least two**), similar to our content map example on the following pages.

Blog

☐ **Editorial Calendar** (create an editorial calendar, outlining key topics/eye catching headlines):

January Topics

- *"How to Build a Business You Love"*
- *"3 Mistakes Your Web Developer Isn't Telling You"*
- *"Why Your Customers Hate Clutter"*
- *"Last Minute Deals to Get Your Kids this Summer"*

February Topics

- *"Which Snow Blower Will Make it Through the Winter"*
- *"Losing Sight of What Matters—Life as a New Mom"*
- *"Sticking to Your Guns and Avoiding Negotiating"*
- *"5 Keys to Having a Six Figure Business"*

☐ **Same Day Weekly Post** (build expectation)
- *Post according to your website analytics to see on average which day results in the highest traffic.*

☐ **Publish Link to New Blog Post on Social Channels** (drive social following back to your website for added search engine optimization value)
- *LinkedIn groups, profile, and company page*
- *Facebook, Twitter, Google+, Pinterest, etc.*
- *Social bookmarking sites*

☐ **Monthly Aggregated Blog Post Email Notification** (designed like LinkedIn Pulse to drive traffic back to website for past blogs)

White Paper

☐ **Publish Quarterly**

☐ **Post on Website and Social Pages**

☐ **Use in Social Campaign** (to drive Facebook likes, downloads, email list opt-in etc.)

Video/Webinar/Slideshare/Infographics/Podcasts

- ☐ **Publish Quarterly**

- ☐ **Record Presentations and Post Video/Transcription on Website, YouTube, and Social Pages**

- ☐ **Add Link to Media in Newsletter**

- ☐ **Publish on Slideshare/Brainshark**

Case Studies

- ☐ **Publish Quarterly**

- ☐ **Post on Blog, Website, and Social Pages**

- ☐ **Use Case studies in Auto Responder Campaign** (for sales funnel engagement)

Guest Posting

- ☐ **Post New material on Outside Sites Besides Company Website**
  - *LinkedIn*
  - *Industry-specific magazines and sites*

And now, it's time to get growing!

Growing Your Family

Marketing, like marriage, is a marathon not a sprint. It takes patience and compromise. And if you grow your family too fast (like getting a puppy and having a baby at the *same time!*) it could easily overwhelm you before it's even had a chance to be successful.

Start small—take baby steps. Grow a plant. Rescue a puppy. Then raise a child. And, over time your marketing will develop into a comprehensive and dynamic content strategy that works together seamlessly—you just need to commit to taking the first step, plan well, and grow slowly!

As marketing content creators, it's Aliste's job to know exactly what to write about and where to post for our clients so that they can have the necessary means to grow at an effective pace for success. To achieve that, we create an in-depth content marketing plan for our clients. And (drum roll please!) we've decided to gift you with that plan, here, just for popping your marketing cherry and jumping into the new marketing world with us!

So, hooray—you've done it! Welcome to marketinghood.

Work It Out

Now it's time to think about quality content control. Answer these questions to help you establish which two platforms your business should start out using:

What's your conversation style(s)?

a) I keep it short and sweet.

b) I love hashing out all the details so there's nothing lost in between the lines.

c) A picture tells a thousand words.

d) Who needs words or pictures when you've got video?

What's your technological status?

a) Surfs Up….Online that is! Love to surf the internet for new things and articles.

b) I would be perfectly fine if I never had to look at a computer again.

c) I know how to get from point A to point B but can only scratch the surface as to what my computer and internet could fully offer.

d) My main networking tool is the internet.

Who do your services/products benefit?

a) Teens and young adults who want the newest and coolest items.

b) Families that want an experience.

c) Women who love to share where they are, what they purchased, and their opinions.

d) Professionals who are looking to connect and grow their business/knowledge.

What contact information do you have access to?

a) I collect emails, names, and additional information from all my customers/clients/contacts.

b) Just the networking or professional groups I am a part of.

c) Just my friends and family…I think.

d) Every time I meet someone I connect with them on Linkedin.

If you answered mostly...

A's: Begin connecting with your audience on the more conversational platforms such as Twitter and Facebook.

B's: Generate original content in the form of blogs and email marketing to build your credibility and Search Engine Optimization. Check out sites like Constant Contact for email marketing and Wordpress for a blogging platform (just make sure your business name is part of the blog URL.)

C's: You agree that images sell your business and products so get involved on Pinterest and Instagram to engage with your audience and encourage your content to be shared via images.

D's: You're trying to get in front of business professionals who value your opinion, content, and level of professionalism. Begin building your LinkedIn profile, join LinkedIn groups and start to think about recording that next webinar to put on your You-Tube channel.

Work It Out / Sum It Up

CHAPTER 1

CHAPTER 2

CHAPTER 3

CHAPTER 4

CHAPTER 5

Once you've completed the above chapters' **Work It Out** pages, print or collect them together before answering the following:

What is my objective? I need readers, prospects, and clients to do what in order to achieve my goal?

☐ Click here to read

☐ Register here

☐ Donate

☐ Buy now

☐ Share

☐ Call us

☐ Schedule a call

☐ Other _____

What campaign will achieve my objective?

☐ To welcome or thank new customers, clients, donors, etc.

☐ Discussion/ round table/ mastermind group.

☐ Promotions and offers.

☐ Event invitations and registration.

☐ Surveys or polls.

☐ Donations and fundraising.

☐ Other _____

How can we tell our story?

☐ How we started.

☐ What's new in the business and the impact on audience?

☐ Opinion piece on industry news.

☐ Other _____

What channels will you use to reach target clients to take action?

- ☐ Social media
- ☐ Direct mail
- ☐ Email campaigns
- ☐ Phone calls
- ☐ Television or radio
- ☐ Other _____

How will you measure the responses?

- ☐ Google analytics for website traffic
- ☐ Email campaign clicks
- ☐ Number of event registrants
- ☐ Amount donated
- ☐ Social shares
- ☐ Other _____

Based on your answers above and the **Work It Out** sheets from each chapter, finish strong with these last five **To Do's** to making it happen for your business.

1) Where is your ideal client?
2) Post your swoon worthy 'Ask' on our Twitter page.
3) Tell your story. Spread the word by submitting it to our blog **mystory@alistemarketing.com**.
4) Create the "wow" experience and stick to it!
5) Pull off the Band-Aid and start somewhere, even if it is just sending an email campaign to your friends and family!

And remember: Marketing is something that is constantly changing, growing, and evolving—just like your business. When you stray or lose focus remember to revisit these **Work It Out** sections and identify the who, what, where, and how of your mission. With these four questions in your corner, you are destined for success.

Keep on building, wooing, searching, and sharing your story as you pop your marketing cherry!

January

Content Marketing Calendar

Popping Your Marketing Cherry   #PopIt

Sunday	Monday	Tuesday	Wednesday	Thursday	Friday	Saturday
					1 All blog content received from writers, edited and imagery selected	**2**
3 Create Editorial Calendar for first quarter.	**4** Motivational Monday social media posts	**5** Blog Post #1: Creating a business you love	**6** Event Promotion or quote of the week on social media	**7** Monthly Email Campaign draft created	**8** Fun Friday social media posts	**9**
10	**11** Motivational Monday social media posts	**12** Blog Post #2: 3 Mistakes you already made on your website	**13** Event Promotion or quote of the week on social media	**14** Work on case study or e-book content	**15** Fun Friday social media posts	**16**
17	**18** Motivational Monday social media posts	**19** Blog Post #3: 6 Reasons your clients hate clutter	**20** Event Promotion or quote of the week on social media	**21** Distribute Monthly Email Campaign	**22** Fun Friday social media posts	**23**
24	**25** Motivational Monday social media posts	**26** Blog Post #4: Getting the dream client	**27** Event Promotion or quote of the week on social media	**28** Respond to all messages, reviews, comments and shares on social media	**29** Fun Friday social media posts	**30**
31 Collect Monthly Insight Report						

www.ingramcontent.com/pod-product-compliance
Lightning Source LLC
Chambersburg PA
CBHW050523210326
41520CB00012B/2410